MODERNBLUES
SLIDEGUITAR

Master The Art of Fusion Slide Blues Guitar in Standard Tuning

ALLENHINDS

FUNDAMENTALCHANGES

Modern Blues Slide Guitar

Master The Art of Fusion Slide Blues Guitar in Standard Tuning

ISBN: 978-1-78933-455-5

Published by **www.fundamental-changes.com**

Copyright © 2024 Allen Hinds

Edited by Tim Pettingale

www.fundamental-changes.com

Join our free Facebook Community of Cool Musicians

www.facebook.com/groups/fundamentalguitar

Instagram: **FundamentalChanges**

For over 350 Free Guitar Lessons with Videos Check Out

www.fundamental-changes.com

Cover Image Copyright: Author photo used by permission.

Contents

Introduction

Welcome to my second book with Fundamental Changes, exploring the language of modern blues in the context of slide guitar. This book is all about playing slide in *standard tuning*, so let me take a moment to explain why I prefer that approach to the various open tunings.

The origins of electric slide guitar come from the pedal steel and Dobro – instruments that are usually tuned to open chords. While they undoubtedly produce a beautiful sound, they have their limitations – especially if we want to play in lots of different keys, or if we want to go outside harmonically in our improvisation. Open tunings also have their own set of patterns on guitar that we must learn if we want to master them, and this means having to set aside the fretboard knowledge we already have.

As a young player I was greatly influenced by Duane Allman (who played slide in open tuning and occasionally standard tuning), but for the reasons stated above, it made sense to me to stick with standard tuning and make a few alterations to my technique to get the best out of it.

Lots of other players have gone down this same road. Using standard tuning allows them to access the expressive qualities of slide guitar when they need it, but quickly switch back to a conventional playing style, without the need to retune or pick up a different guitar.

One of the keys to making slide playing work in standard tuning is having a good picking hand muting technique. We'll work on this in Chapter One, where I'll also share other tips and tricks that I use. I'll also show you some foundational licks that I use all the time. You can think of these as the *building blocks* of standard tuning slide vocabulary. Then, in chapters 2-5, we'll learn tons more slide vocabulary as we break down and analyze four modern blues solos with various feels.

By the end of this book, you should be equipped with plenty of modern blues slide ideas that will work in the context of straight ahead blues, funk-influenced blues, and fusion-oriented blues rock. Let's get started and work on incorporating this expressive technique into your soloing repertoire.

Have fun with it!

Allen

Get the Audio

The audio files for this book are available to download for free from **www.fundamental-changes.com**. The link is in the top right-hand corner. Click "Download Audio" and choose your instrument. Select the title of this book from the menu, and complete the form to get your audio.

We recommend that you download the files directly to your computer (not to your tablet or phone) and extract them there before adding them to your media library. If you encounter any difficulty, we provide technical support within 24 hours via the contact form.

For over 350 free guitar lessons with videos check out:

www.fundamental-changes.com

Join our free Facebook Community of Cool Musicians

www.facebook.com/groups/fundamentalguitar

Tag us for a share on Instagram: **FundamentalChanges**

Chapter One – Core Techniques

In this chapter we'll lay the foundation for what's to come in subsequent chapters. Later, we will break down four full-length solos and use them to learn some fusion-blues slide guitar vocabulary. But first, we need to practice the right-hand muting technique that lies at the heart of playing slide in open tuning. Plus, I want to show you a few other cool tricks and licks that will elevate your technique.

Before we get started, we need to talk about two things: your guitar and your slide!

You'll often hear players say, "You can't play slide unless you have a high action."

In one sense that's true.

If *all* you did was play side, then it would make sense to have a high-ish action on your guitar to eliminate unwanted fret noise.

But I've been playing for many years and I manage to play slide with a pretty low action, which means I can switch between playing slide and regular playing whenever I need to. It's just a matter of having a solid picking hand muting technique and a delicate touch with the fretting hand.

If you already prefer to play with a fairly high action, then we're all good. But if, like me, you like to play with a pretty low action, I'm here to reassure you that you can master slide with your existing setup – which in the end will give you the freedom to switch between slide and conventional playing in a heartbeat.

Now onto the slide…

I grew up in Alabama listening to Duane Allman, who mostly played in open tunings, but also played slide in standard tuning (check out the songs *Mountain Jam* and *Dreams*). He was a big influence on me, so I naturally gravitated toward the glass slide that he used.

Over the years I've tried a few different ones – standard steel and also super heavy brass ones – but I've always come back to the glass slide. In fact, I actually use a Pyrex slide, which has the same feel and tone of glass, but is much lighter.

This is important, because the lighter slide doesn't clunk against the frets too much, and this helps me with keeping the action low on my guitar; I can use a very light touch to produce the notes. Ultimately, you need to go with the slide that feels most comfortable to you and produces the kind of tone you like, but this is my approach.

What about guitar tone?

Tone is a thing of preference. Speaking for myself, I always switch to the bridge pickup for slide work and roll back the treble a little, so that it's not overly cutting. The bridge pickup is my preference because I use only my fingers when playing slide, and it restores some of the brightness to the sound.

I also think the bridge pickup helps to accentuate the natural harmonics that slide playing brings out, and it sounds to me like the best way to get close to that Duane Allman tone that I love!

Getting used to wearing the slide

If you've not played much slide until now, and you're here because it's a style you want to get into, the first thing to do is just get used to wearing the slide. It's normal for it to feel a little awkward at first, so that's the first thing to get over.

Then we have the question of which finger to put the slide on...

There are a couple of different approaches and everyone has their reasons for which finger they prefer. For me, it's the third (ring) finger.

Part of the reason for that is definitely Duane Allman's influence. But I also discovered that wearing the slide on the third finger makes it easier to turn the slide sideways (a technique I use to move between major and minor 3rd intervals). Plus, it allows me to keep a couple of fingers free to play notes below the slide. Both are techniques we'll look at and use throughout the book.

Getting a feel for slide notes

Once you feel comfortable wearing the slide, it's good to get used to playing notes on just one string.

The first thing players often do when they pick up a slide is to play the fast vibrato idea in bars 1-2 below, sliding in from below the notes... of course!

It's one of the most obvious and cool things you can do with a slide, but it is a cliché.

What interests me more is the expressive potential of slide guitar, and how it's possible to achieve a vocal-like quality with the slide.

The sound that appeals to me, which I always try to go for, is to replicate the singing quality of the pedal steel, like the very simple phrase I play in bars 3-4.

Listen to the audio example and try it out now!

Example 1a

Achieving a vocal quality in our slide work is much harder than playing flashy, wide vibrato licks. Why? Because we need to be much more accurate with our intonation.

It can sometimes be harder to hear when a note is in tune or not when playing slide, so a good way to practice this is to turn on your tuner while you're playing.

Often, I'll just slide into and hold one note (as in Example 1b), applying some very subtle vibrato, and watch my tuner to see when I'm playing sharp or flat.

Play Example 1b, but then spend a good chunk of time practicing this with different notes in different places on the neck. Keep your tuner on and be aware of what note you're aiming for.

(I suspect you'll know this already, but when we play a note with the slide, we have to position the slide exactly above the fret wire, not in the middle of the fret).

Work on this for a while and you'll soon begin to develop an understanding of what it *feels* like when you're playing in tune, plus your ear will improve too.

Example 1b

Don't shortchange the idea of practicing single notes and getting them perfectly in tune, because this is a very important part of polishing your technique. But when you feel ready, the next step is to play scales or scalic phrases on one string and aim to get all the notes perfectly in tune.

Play through Example 1c. Don't worry about playing it to a tempo, just focus on getting every note perfectly in tune.

Example 1c

I find that the direct contact I have with the strings, by just using the fingers of my picking hand, gives me much more control over the expression and emotion I want to inject into phrases.

We'll dig into right-hand muting technique in more detail in a moment, but in terms of picking the strings, I recommend a fingerstyle version of hybrid picking.

I pick downward with my thumb, and pluck upward on the adjacent strings with my first, second and third fingers.

Try this by playing Example 1d. Pluck downward with your thumb on the D string, upward with your first finger on the G string, and upward with your second finger on the B string.

If you're a strictly plectrum player, it might take a little while to get used to this approach, but controlling the strings with separate fingers like this is key in minimizing unwanted string noise, and it gives a clarity to the notes that we *do* want to hear.

In bar four, when you slide up to the 17th fret, really make that note sing by holding it perfectly in tune, then add the vibrato afterward. I like to slide up to notes slowly, with no vibrato, then add a little backward and forward shake with the slide to simulate that vocal quality.

For practice, take any simple pentatonic shape and work on your picking hand finger coordination across the strings. Work on playing some of your favorite licks, slide style.

Example 1d

Picking hand muting

We've looked at some tips for achieving good intonation and controlling notes with the slide, but the most important technique for playing slide, to get a great sound and make it as musical as it can be, is picking hand muting.

There are several fretting hand slide techniques we'll want to use where, if good muting is not applied, the sound will quickly get out of hand and there will be tons of extraneous string noise.

For example, one thing I like to do is to angle the slide to play a minor 3rd interval.

In Example 1e, think of the parallel notes at the 14th fret as your home base, where the slide is positioned straight across the frets. Place your slide here, at the 14th, to begin with.

Now rotate your fretting hand wrist slightly, in the direction of your neck pickup, so that your slide angle upward across the frets.

Pivoting your wrist like this allows the slide to sit at an angle over the 15th/16th frets.

Now pluck the strings simultaneously with your thumb and first finger, and rotate your wrist back so that the slide returns to the 14th fret.

That's a long description, but try it and you'll get it immediately.

We'll use this technique throughout the solos that follow, so spend some time practicing it, and getting the notes in tune.

Example 1e

Another technique we'll want to use (and a good reason for wearing the slide on the third finger) is to play fretted notes behind the slide using our spare fingers.

This is another technique that can feel a little alien at first, but persistent practice will make it feel comfortable, and it can give you "best of both worlds" options for creating melodic lines.

With this technique, we don't move the slide. It stays in position while we play other notes around it, and we don't move it until we have to.

Listen to the audio for this example, then give it a go. It begins with the slide positioned at the 9th fret. After playing the 9th, lift the slide slightly and play the 8th fret with your first finger. Then put the slide back on the strings to play the 9th fret again.

After that, you'll shift position so that the slide is positioned over the 12th fret. Notes at the 9th and 10th frets will be played with the first finger behind the slide.

Example 1f

Now that you've tried the technique, how can you go about muting the strings to make these ideas sound clean?

I designate one picking hand finger per string.

I use my thumb and fingers 1, 2 and 3, and don't use my pinkie at all.

This means that when playing phrases, my picking hand will move up and down a little, depending on what string I'm playing on.

Practice sitting your picking hand on the strings as described for a minute.

Your thumb will look after the E, A and D bass strings, and your fingers will fall in line underneath it on adjacent strings.

Practice hopping across the strings and playing notes on different string combinations to get a feel for it.

It's a picking and muting technique, all rolled into one.

Now try this little arpeggio exercise.

Your thumb will be resting on the D string. The side of your hand will mute the A and E bass strings.

Play a fast rake from the D to B string with your thumb, first finger and second finger. Then pick back down to the D string. You can also just slide into the 12th fret of the B string and pick downwards (bar three).

Make sure that you're muting the un-played strings as effectively as you can.

For practice, just play the figure in bar three. When you play the B string 12th fret, you'll pluck it with your second finger. As you do so, your other fingers should be resting on the strings around it, muting them.

When you move to the G string, you'll play that with your first finger, and your second finger must drop back onto the B string to mute it.

When you play the D string with the thumb, your first finger will drop back onto the G string to mute it.

Hopefully, you can see the mechanical pattern your picking hand must follow.

Keep practicing this so that it becomes a habit to mute any string that is not currently being played. With time, you'll become more adept at only sounding the notes you want to be heard.

Example 1g

Ok, let's pause for a moment…

You've now got some foundational techniques under your fingers, but don't rush ahead too soon. Mastering these techniques is what will set you apart from other players: the quality of your intonation, the cleanness of your picking/muting, and your ability with note control.

Work on these three elements in your practice times, just by sitting with the guitar and playing simple repetitive phrases. Becoming adept with a hybrid picking approach will be the most challenging aspect. Josh Smith once told me that when he began hybrid picking, he'd just sit with his guitar unplugged, watching TV, and persistently hybrid pick banjo rolls on three strings with his thumb and first and second fingers, until it was second nature and he didn't have to think about it anymore. Try doing the same, but with your slide on the strings.

Moving on, let's begin to look at some simple licks and cool ideas we can use.

Example 1h is a movement that is foundational to my slide guitar vocabulary, influenced by Ry Cooder. The very simple idea here is to slide down on one string, then slide up on an adjacent string.

In bar two, you'll slide down to the C note on the B string from above, then slide up to the B note on the G string from below.

You can think of this idea like a motif (a repeating musical idea) and apply it all over the fretboard. It's a way of playing just two notes to achieve vocal-like articulation.

This example works over a G7 chord and the notes come from the G Mixolydian scale.

This is also a good lick to practice your picking hand muting skills!

Example 1h

You can play this motif anywhere and also adapt it slightly if you like.

This line uses the idea while descending in thirds.

Example 1i

Now let's try a few licks that require us to angle the slide.

This line includes the angled slide movement in bar two, as a natural part of a bigger idea.

Example 1j

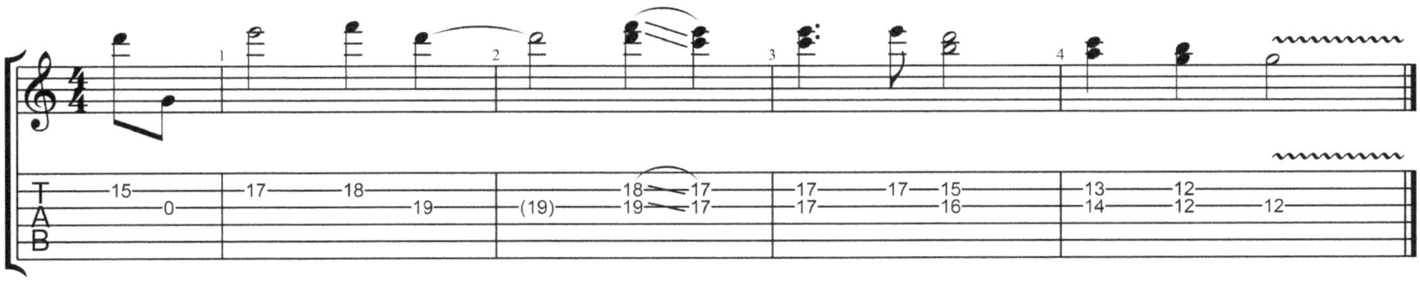

Here's another angled slide lick for you to try. In bar one, start with the slide angled so that it covers the 18th/19th frets, then straighten it to play the notes on the 17th fret.

In bar two, practice moving the slide while keeping it angled.

In bar three, reverse the process by beginning with the slide parallel to play the notes at the 12th fret, then angle the slide to play the notes at the 11th & 12th frets.

Keep the slide angled to play the notes at the 10th and 12th in bar four, then straighten the slide again for the rest of the bar.

Take your time with this and get the notes perfectly in tune.

Example 1k

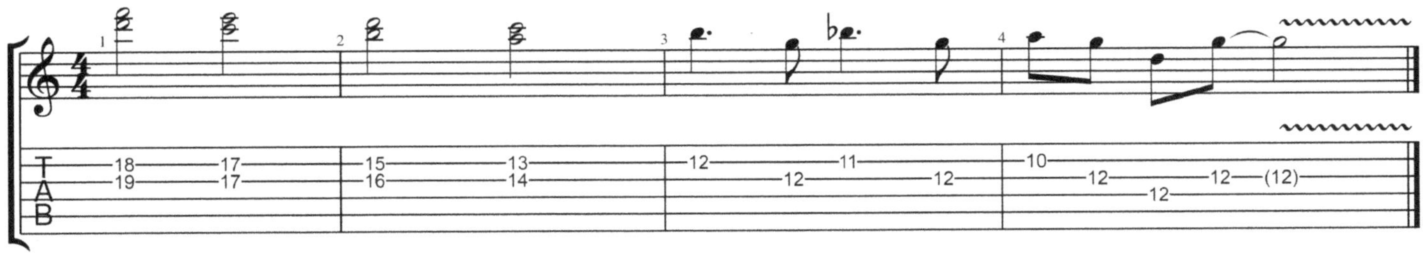

The next example combines the techniques of angling the pick and sliding on adjacent strings.

Example 1l

Here's a fast lick that descends rapidly on parallel strings, and in bar two we play a fast upward slide from way down on the neck.

Example 1m

Next, try this bluesy lick that includes notes played behind the slide. Work through it very slowly at first, and figure out your fingering and picking.

In bar two, keep the slide steady at the 5th fret and lightly fret the note on the G string, 4th fret, with your first finger. Repeat the process with the slide at the 12th, fretting on the 10th with your first finger.

Example 1n

The next example also uses behind the slide fretted notes for a lick in the high register.

This can be a tricky technique to master, so work through this idea slowly, focusing on achieving good intonation and good picking hand muting to control string noise.

Check out the audio example to hear exactly how it should sound.

Example 1o

Example 1p brings together several of the core techniques we've been looking at.

I played this example in free time and Levi Clay, our valiant transcriber, has done his best to turn it into readable notation/TAB that makes sense.

But don't worry too much about trying to play it in time, because it's grabbing the ideas that is important here.

Consider this an exercise to work on in your practice times. It contains pentatonic scale patterns, notes played behind the slide, and sliding on adjacent strings.

Example 1p

Example 1q is a pentatonic scale lick that combines notes played with the slide and fretted notes behind it.

In this instance, because it's a straight ascending lick, I'm plucking everything using just my thumb and first finger and moving them across the strings.

Example 1q

Here's that pentatonic exercise developed into a call and response lick with more articulation added.

Example 1r

Next up, an emotive lick constructed entirely from the downward slide idea.

Example 1s

This bluesy lick, based around a tonal center of D, uses a chromatic descending motif idea.

This is the type of lick I play a lot, because it combines standard blues slide vocabulary with a more modern fusion-blues "outside-inside" approach.

Example 1t

The next line incorporates a repeating triplet motif that I like to play, and you'll see this crop up in the solos.

This is played with the thumb and fingers 1 and 2. It's executed like a Country banjo roll, with the thumb plucking downward and the fingers picking upward.

Example 1u

Lastly, here's one more chance to practice the angled slide approach and the emotive technique of sliding into a note from above.

This is also a good test for your picking hand muting technique. You'll need to work carefully to control the open string notes in bar four and minimize string noise.

Example 1v

Now that you have the fundamental techniques under your fingers, continue to practice and refine them. In the chapters that follow we'll focus on soloing in the context of modern blues and add some ideas to your vocabulary.

Chapter Two – Slow Blues Study

With some fundamental techniques in place, we can now begin to look at developing our soloing language for slide guitar in standard tuning. As well as applying the techniques we've learned, we'll now also consider note/scale choices, phrasing, and how to incorporate runs/scale sequences. The aim is to help you develop a vocabulary you can draw on in real musical situations.

We'll start with an easy vehicle for us to improvise and experiment over – a simple three-chord blues in G Major, played at slow tempo.

The simplicity of this structure will give you plenty of opportunity to check your intonation on long-held notes, and practice your vocal phrasing.

This blues is played with a 12/8 feel and begins with a four-bar intro. The band play two bars, then there is a two-bar stop during which the soloist can play an opening phrase. The 12-bar blues structure begins properly in Example 2b.

In bar one, we start simply by targeting the root note of the G9 chord. Check that your intonation is good as you slide into and hold the G note at the 5th fret.

This initial note bleeds into the next phrase. You'll hear on the audio that I only pick the F note at the 3rd fret and the rest of the phrase is accomplished just by moving the slide.

The open D string is heard subtly and I make that note sound by rolling the slide off the string briefly – a bit like a pull-off – then rolling it back on, to slide up to the 5th.

Often in blues soloing, major and minor tonalities are blurred and players freely switch between them. So, although we're playing over a dominant chord with a major 3rd, all the notes of the opening phrase are from the G Minor Pentatonic scale (G Bb C D F) which has a minor 3rd. It's one of the quirks of the blues that we all love and accept.

In bar two, we switch to the G Mixolydian scale (G A B C D E F). Notice at the end of bar one that we play an E approach note that leads into the F at the beginning of bar three. F is the b7 of the G9 chord.

In bar three, you'll need to roll the slide off the string again to play the open D string. When playing the double-stop on the bottom strings, be sure to mute the D string until you're ready to play it.

Example 2a

As the first chorus of the 12-bar begins, we kick things off with a lick that highlights the root of the G chord, moving up to its 3rd (B).

My strategy for this lick was to use the G Mixolydian scale (which has a major 3rd, B) and occasionally "borrow" the minor third (Bb) from the G Minor Pentatonic scale (as in the end of bar two on the B string, 11th fret).

Introducing this technically dissonant note is the essence of the blues.

It also gives the line a bluesy vibe when we highlight the b7 (F) of the G9 chord at the end of bar three/ beginning of bar four.

Example 2b

As we move to the C9, we spell out the harmony by playing chord tones in 6ths. At the beginning of bar one, the notes are the 3rd and 5th of C9.

We slide down chromatically to the 3rd fret, where the notes are F and D.

The D note is the 9th of C9. The F note isn't in the chord, but is actually the 11th of C9. So, we haven't gone outside the harmony here, we're just playing extended notes.

Let's focus on the phrase in the bar two, which is all about the articulation. In the first half of the phrase, you'll slide into the 5th fret of the G string from below, then down to the 3rd fret.

You then need to quickly slide into the 9th fret from below and to the 3rd fret from above. Listen to the audio, then practice that four-note motif until you're able to pitch it accurately every time. Inject plenty of emotion!

At the end of bar four, move your slide back and forth between the 13th and 15th frets to play the repeating phrase.

Example 2c

Bar one of this example is a continuation of the phrase that was played in bar four of Example 2c, as we hit the root of the D9 chord on the B string, 15th fret.

You're probably realizing already that some of these licks stand or fall on the quality of the articulation with which they're played.

Whether you're sliding into a note from above or below, always strive for accuracy with your intonation and don't add any vibrato until you've nailed the pitch.

Depending on the phrase, this can sometimes be a split second, but the more you practice accurate fretting, the more natural you'll become at it. Remember that we're fretting notes with the slide positioned directly above the fret wire, not in the middle of the fret!

Example 2d

Example 2e picks up where 2d left off, in the final bar before the 12-bar sequence starts over.

The most difficult part of this line is the ascending run in the pickup bar, which moves into the highly articulated single string work over the G9 chord, so let's break that down.

In the pickup bar, place your slide parallel to fret 17. You'll play the notes in brackets with the first finger of the fretting hand, behind the slide.

Lift your first finger up and down while keeping the slide in place to get the pattern of alternating notes.

The challenging part of this phrase is the fact that after the first four notes we speed up (notated as 1/16th note triplets). Listen to the audio a few times to get the phrasing in your head.

The next challenging part is the line in bar one, where we work our way up to a high D note on fret 22.

The 12/8 time signature has a naturally swinging triplet feel, but here we need to play with a straight, lazy phrasing that cuts against the beat with a "4 over 3" feel.

It's like the notes are inching their way up to that D, rather than playing in time!

In the second half of the phrase, only pick the note at the 20th fret, and just move the slide to generate the other notes.

In bars 3-4, the brackets represent tied notes. Again, carefully check out the audio to get the phrasing down. In bar four, this is just "random slide noise", which you can approach however you want!

Example 2e

In Example 2f we introduce a new technique that can be used as a special effect: playing harmonics while using the slide.

Yes, you can still include harmonics in your playing, and the addition of the slide means that you can also move harmonics around the neck for a really cool, attention grabbing effect.

Just as in regular playing, you can use natural harmonics (as we're doing here) or artificial harmonics.

In bar two, pick the harmonic at the 5th fret by touching lightly with your finger over the fret wire. Then bring the slide from behind the nut and quickly slide up the neck to raise the pitch of the harmonic.

Artificial harmonics can be accomplished with the slide held in place over a fret, while we pick 12 frets higher.

Sliding harmonics up into the higher register can be a lot of fun, as it takes the note beyond the normal harmonic range of the instrument.

Take some time to get this technique down.

Example 2f

In the final four bars of the 12-bar progression, you'll start by playing a "lazy" sounding phrase that mixes sliding into notes from below and above.

Aim to play mostly behind the beat here and you'll capture the right feel, but the last note of bar one is played *before* the beat and left hanging.

At the beginning of bar two, you'll need to move smoothly between the 17th and 20th frets to play this little lick. It's a version of the "sliding down on one string and up on an adjacent string" movement we've practiced, though here I didn't slide up into the 20th fret, I just moved there and picked the note.

You'll also need to get your picking hand muting in place to play this cleanly.

At the end of bar four there is an ascending run that will continue at the beginning of the next example.

Example 2g

Bar one of Example 2h continues the ascending run on the high E string. When you run out of fretboard, you're going to use another new technique: playing notes over the pickups.

With no frets to provide a roadmap, playing beyond the end of the neck is a matter of using your ears to pitch each note.

There is no visual reference in terms of frets, but if you play slide mostly using the same guitar, you can use other points of reference, such as the edge or middle of the neck pickup, etc.

With practice, you'll soon be able to "extend" your neck to play super high notes, and they are certainly ear catching.

Here, the framework providing the notes is the G Blues scale, but we're including lots of chromatic approach notes here too.

Example 2h

In this example you'll play more notes over the pickups – this time on more than one string, so really use your ears and listen closely to your pitch.

In bars 2-4 you'll play a staple blues slide lick, which is a must-have for your arsenal of phrases. Work out your slide positioning movements to begin with and play it very slowly, with good picking hand muting, before bringing it up to speed.

Example 2i

Here are some more standard blues licks, converted for standard-tuning slide, which navigate the turnaround section of the blues.

We're using the D Mixolydian scale in bar one, and C Mixolydian in bar two.

In bar three over the G9 chord, I used a hybrid scale idea. I used the G Mixolydian scale as my framework, but augmented it by borrowing the Bb note from the G Blues scale.

This results in a scale that contains both a major and a minor 3rd.

If you've never experimented with this idea, I recommend checking it out.

Example 2j

This example begins with a chromatic ascending line in the pickup bar, targeting the G9 chord tone that falls on beat 1 of bar one.

In bar one, the first note (D) is the 5th of G9, and the last note (B) is the 3rd. These notes act like anchors for this chromatic line.

If you play strong chord tones at the beginning and end of a phrase, all sorts of mayhem can take place in between, and it'll still sound like your line is grounded and makes sense!

The idea of using strong chord tones as targets is an essential ingredient of modern sounding, outside-inside playing.

Playing outside doesn't mean playing "wrong notes", rather it's about creating tension with a delayed resolution. Encase a phrase in chord tones and you can get away with a lot of chromatic notes.

Take care to control the string noise when playing the bluesy phrase in bar two.

Example 2k

Over the C9 chord here, we're using the C Mixolydian scale to outline the chord and the phrase ends on the 9th (D).

For the G9, we're using G Mixolydian as our framework again, with a borrowed Bb note, but there are also other chromatic passing notes thrown into the mix.

Example 2l

This final example brings the solo to a conclusion.

In bar one we target a high G note. Over the D9 chord this note represents the 11th.

In bar two, the C9 chord is defined by playing its b7 (Bb) at the beginning of the phrase and its root note at the end.

In bar three we end with an ascending line using our hybrid G Mixolydian scale.

Example 2m

You have the backing track for this tune in your audio download, and I recommend spending lots of time just jamming over it.

Work on your intonation, practice sliding licks on adjacent strings, and work at refining your picking hand muting technique.

Above all, experiment fearlessly and see what happy accidents occur. Grab hold of the licks you like and use them until they become a part of your own slide vocabulary.

When you're confident, here is the entire solo for you to play through. Attempting to learn the whole performance is going to help cement these ideas for you.

Example 2n – Full Solo

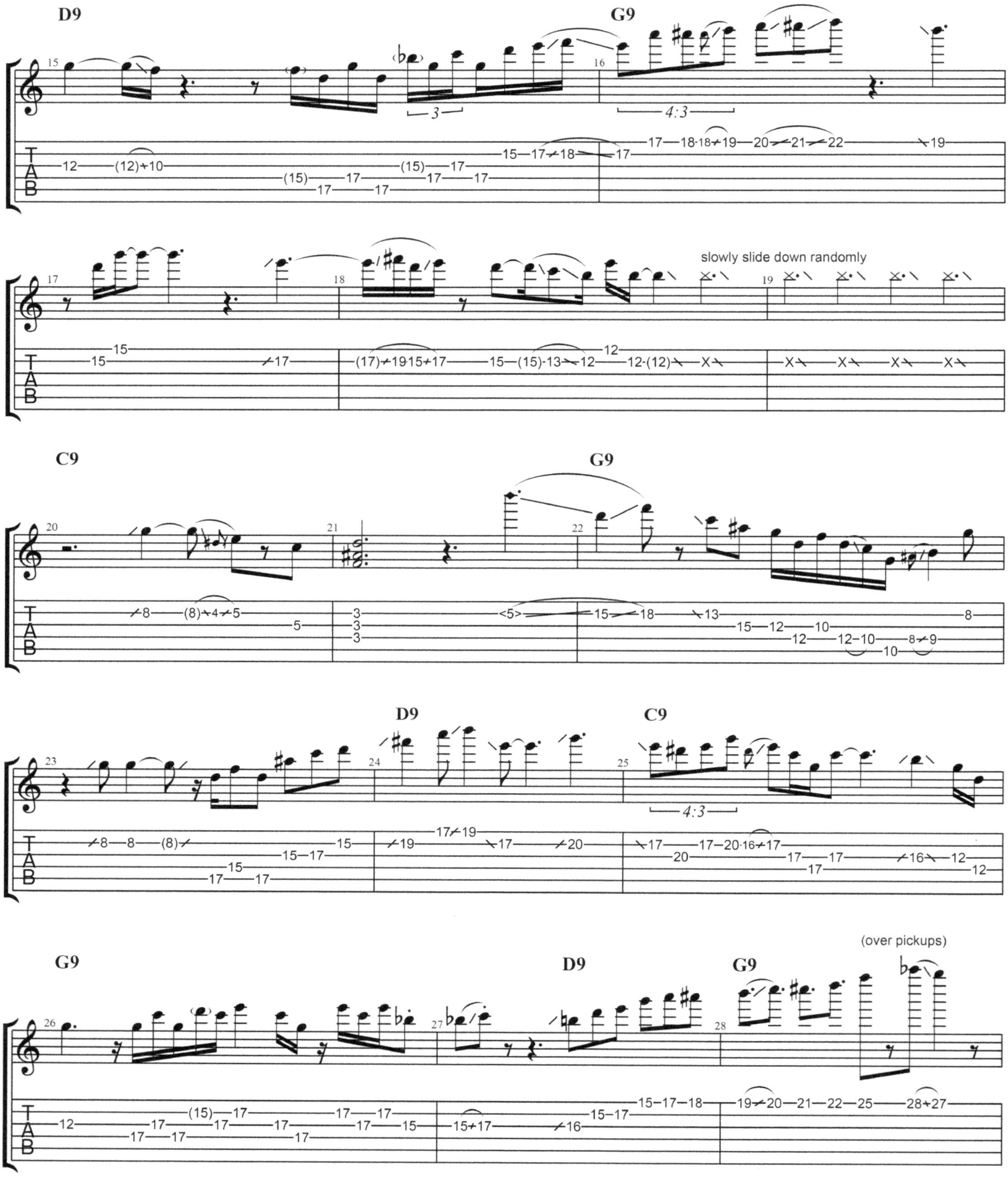
D9
G9
slowly slide down randomly
C9
G9
D9
C9
G9
D9
G9
(over pickups)

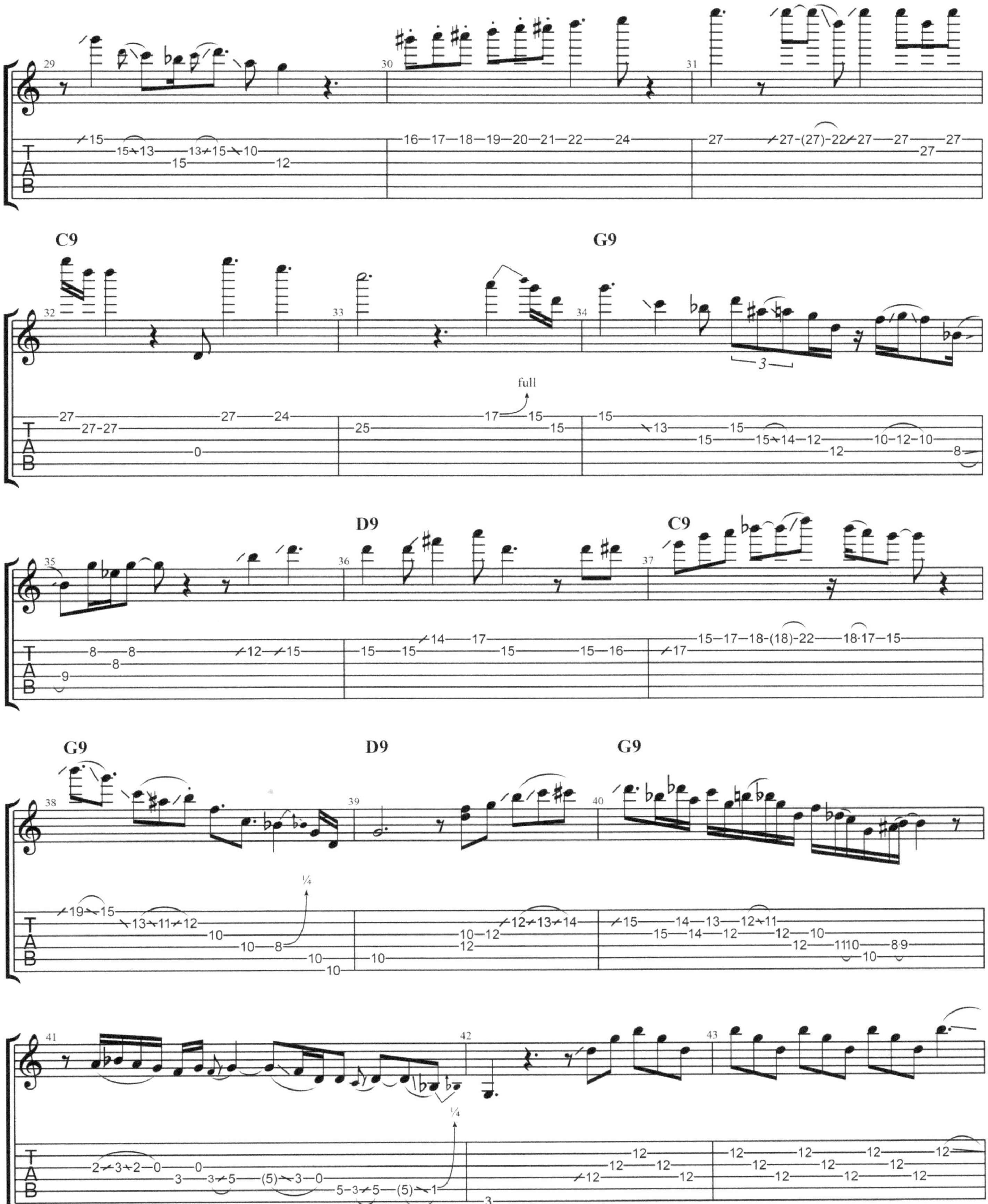
C9
G9
full
D9
C9
G9
D9
G9
¼
¼

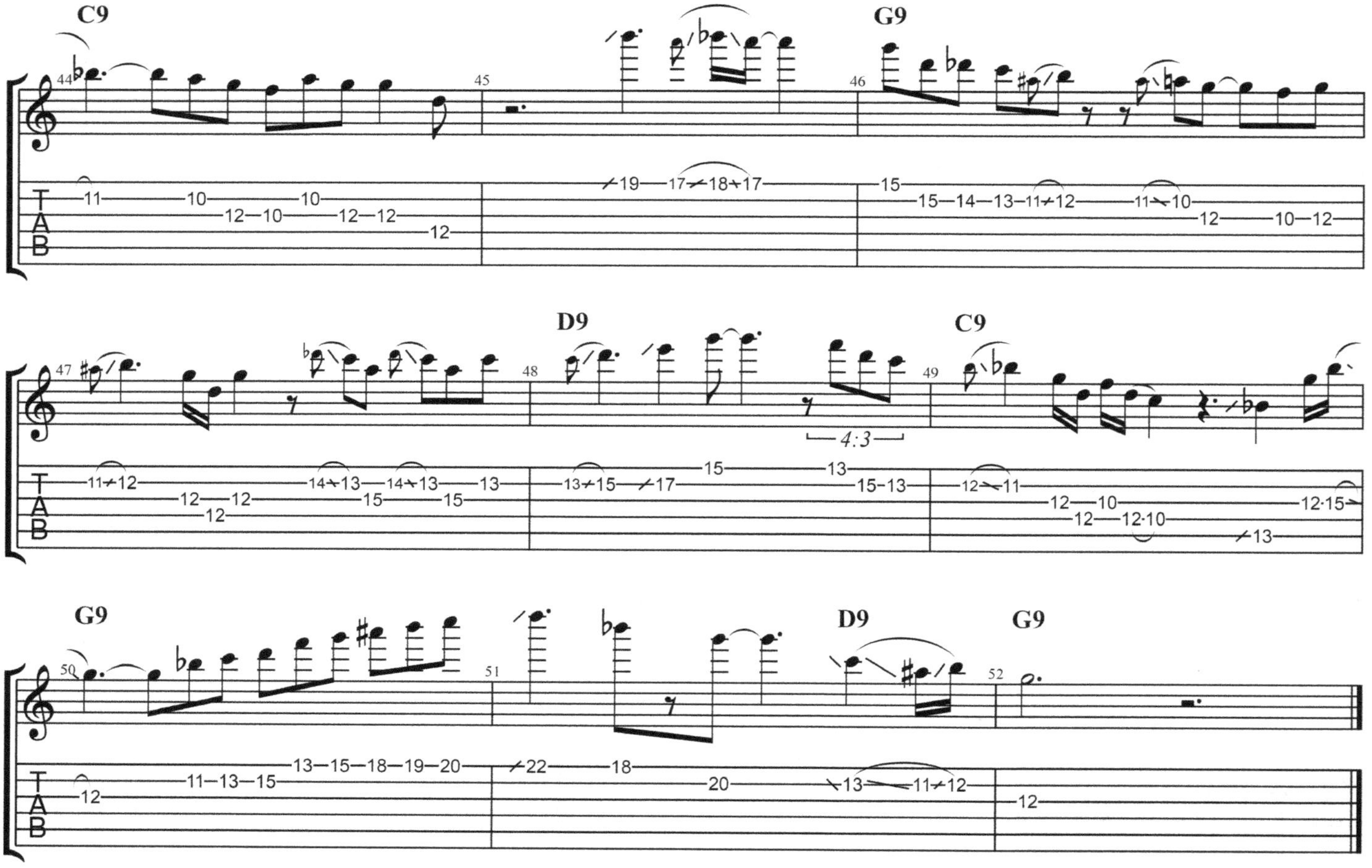
C9
G9
D9
C9
4:3
G9
D9
G9

Chapter Three – Blues Rock Study

Next, we turn our attention to soloing over a blues-rock tune in the key of D. Although the overall tonality of this piece suggests we're in D Major, like all blues-rock soloing approaches, we'll be blurring the lines between major and minor.

This means we'll draw from major and minor pentatonic scale ideas, and also use the Mixolydian and Blues scales to compose our melodic lines.

One extra feature of this solo is that I decided to play it in Drop D tuning to add extra depth and power. Just tune your low E string down a whole step to D and you're good to go.

We open the solo with a long slow slide up to the root note of the D chord at the 10th fret of the high E string, and bounce off the 5th (A) on the B string.

In the latter half of bar one, you'll play one of our foundational licks, sliding down on one string and playing a higher note on an adjacent string.

For the rest of this line, we target the root notes of the chords to spell out the changes.

In bar one and the beginning of bar two, the notes comes from the D Blues scale (D F G Ab A C).

In bar two, we switch to the F Mixolydian scale (F G A Bb C D Eb).

At the end of bar four we can play an F power chord at the 3rd fret, as we're in Drop D tuning.

Example 3a

In Drop D tuning we can also play a D power chord using the open bottom three strings, which is a powerful sound and compliments the track.

You'll notice in this example that we "bounce" off open strings at various points in the phrasing. Good fretting hand muting is needed to make sure you minimize string noise when lifting the slide from the strings.

It's tempting when playing slide to go wild and just play the impressive stuff with big slides, but we mustn't lose sight of playing with good phrasing. This line develops a short motif in a question and answer style.

Example 3b

This line continues the motif in the first three bars, then grounds the idea in the fourth bar. Spot the signature lick in the pickup bar, which this time also includes an open string.

The only potentially tricky part of this line is the fingering in bar four.

Play the notes on the 5th fret of the G string and 7th fret of the D string with the slide. Then play the 4th fret of the G string as a fretted note (shown in brackets) with your first finger behind the slide. Jump the slide back up to the 7th fret to play the downward slide into the 5th fret.

Example 3c

Something I like to do, which you'll often hear in my playing, is to build an ascending run from a repeating triplet pattern.

In the pickup bar and bar one of this example, you'll play a 1/16th note triplet pattern, which over the driving 4/4 beat, creates a sense of urgency and momentum.

This phrase uses behind the slide fretting.

In these first two bars, the fretted notes are indicated enclosed in brackets. Position your slide over the 12th fret and hold it there.

In the pickup bar, play the 10th fret of the D string with your first finger, then all notes at the 12th with the slide.

In bar one, play the 11th fret of the G string with your second finger, and use the slide for the notes at the 12th. You'll use the first finger again for fretting at the 10th fret of the B string.

NB: Tied notes are also indicated by brackets! Here we run up against the limitations of TAB/notation software. If you see a single bracketed note, it'll usually mean it is fretted. If you see a bracketed note following on from the same note, it's usually a tied note!

Another technique used in this line is what I'll call "simulated bending". In other words, mimicking a bend using the slide.

In bar two you'll see two notes indicated as 1/4 note bends, but they are just played with the slide.

Rather than actually bending the string, instead we slowly move the slide slightly beyond the fret to simulate the sound of bending the string upward.

This requires control and precision, but when you get it right it sounds just like a blues curl bend.

Example 3d

Here's another lick that uses behind the slide fretting.

In bar one, position the slide over the 15th fret and play the 13th fret notes on the high E with your first finger.

To outline the Bb chord we're playing its 5th (F) and 3rd (D), before resolving the line to the root note. In bar two, we spell out the chord change to G in a similar way.

In bars 3-4 we're shifting between major and minor tonalities over the C chord. The first half of the line uses the C Major Pentatonic scale (C D E G A), which morphs into the C Minor Pentatonic scale (C Eb F G Bb) in the latter half.

Example 3e

In this example, we begin by outlining the Bb chord, playing a D and Bb double-stop (3rd and root), then ascend to the Bb note on the 18th fret of the high E string.

Before the bar ends, we anticipate the coming G chord by changing that Bb to a B (3rd of G).

In bars 3-4 I decided to take a different approach to building a line over the C chord. Our overall tonal center is D, and here I opted for a minor sound using the D Minor scale (D E F G A Bb C) to provide the notes. The first note in bar three is fretted behind the slide.

Example 3f

Example 3g mixes things up rhythmically to keep things interesting in the solo and keep the momentum going.

In bar one we have the 1/16th note triplet pattern. After the lead-in notes, the first grouping of triplets begins on beat 2 of the bar. The second group of six notes begins on beat 3, and the next group of six on beat 4.

In bar three you'll see the now familiar idea of sliding down on one string and playing a higher note on an adjacent string. This repeated phrase is played quickly and most of the emphasis is placed on the fluid-sounding downward slide.

Inject as much emotion as you can into this lick!

Example 3g

The next example is longer and features several of the techniques we've used in this chapter.

In bars 1-2, notes on the G string 7th fret are fretted behind the slide.

In bar two, the 12th to 10th fret double-stop slide is a very convenient way to spell out the G to F change, using the root and 5th of each chord.

In bars 3-5 we drop into the D Minor Pentatonic scale (D F G A C) for most of this line. This idea uses repeating notes to create a kind of loop effect.

We speed things up at the end of bar two with a group of six 1/16th note triplets (the first note of the group is fretted behind the slide), which creates a feeling of urgency going into the high notes on the top string.

When playing the F note on the high E string, we play another simulated bend, pushing the note gradually sharp to emulate a blues curl.

In bars 6-8, as the instruction on the TAB points out, we are playing long slides down the neck, starting on random notes. The notes aren't meant to be clearly heard, we're just going for an effect here and using the unique characteristics of the slide to create a mournful sound.

Example 3h

At the beginning of this line, slide into the 5th fret and leave your first finger resting over the 3rd fret. Play a fretted note on the B string 3rd fret, then slide into the same note on the G string 7th fret.

For the triplet phrase in bar two, notes on the 5th fret of the G string will be fretted behind the slide.

Example 3i

The next section of the tune begins with some blues phrasing from the D Minor Pentatonic scale over the Bb chord. We expand this idea into the full D Minor scale in bar two, so that we can play a bluesy Bb note over the G chord.

For the C chord, on this occasion I played the ascending line with a hybrid scale that combines notes from C Mixolydian and C Minor Pentatonic.

Rather than viewing these as two distinct scales or sounds, I tend see them as a pool of available notes from which I can choose, and I'll look for those colorful notes that are in easy reach of the shape I'm playing at any given moment.

In bar four, after the 1/16th note triplet phrase, the notes on the high E and G strings (G and Bb) are the 5th and 7th of a C7 chord. I slide these notes down a whole step (a typical blues move) to create some tension. The result is an F note, which is the 11th of the chord, and an Ab, which is its #5.

Example 3j

The main challenge in this next example is the complex line over the C chord in bars 3-4.

This time, we are using the C Mixolydian scale for note choices. The line sounds more involved than it is because we are sliding into certain notes from above.

Work out your fingering/slide movements before attempting the line.

Example 3k

To bring a different flavor to this line, we're starting out with a D major sound. In bar one we begin by highlighting an F# note – the major 3rd of the D chord, followed by its 11th (G).

Playing the root of the G chord and the 5th (C) of the F chord to follow, doesn't alter the major feel of the line.

In bar three, I'm thinking of this descending line on the B string as more of a pattern than a scale – although I had a D7 chord in mind, and this most closely represents the D Mixolydian scale.

The important notes are at the beginning and end: we start on the b7 (C) of the chord and end on its root.

Example 31

This next example seeks to keep the interest and momentum high by introducing rhythmic variety into the phrases.

There is a lot to think about in this line as it uses behind the slide fretting, heavy articulation on the slides, and rhythmic variety.

Throughout bar one, the rhythms get faster, moving from a 1/4 note to 1/16th notes, then into the six-note phrase that combines 1/16th and 1/32nd notes.

This is a great way of giving a line a sense of urgency and pushing forward. Listen to the audio carefully to understand the timing that is required.

In bar two, the slides from below into the notes on the B string should be heavy and exaggerated – they are there for effect, to introduce a dynamic sense of upward motion. They are also aiming for a target note – the F at the beginning of bar three, suggesting a Dm chord.

To play the fast lick that spans the end of bar three/beginning of bar four, start with the slide across fret 22. Pick the B string and slide down to the 20th, then back up to the 22nd and pick the note on the G string.

Throughout this lick, you'll just move the slide back and forth between these frets, picking on adjacent strings.

It's easier than it sounds – promise!

Example 3m

In contrast to that busy line, here we stretch out the notes to get the most from each one.

There are lots of high notes on the top string in bars 1-2 and it's easy to lose accuracy with your intonation in this region of the neck, where small movements have a great effect.

Use your ears to ensure you're sounding the note you want, and hold back on the vibrato until your pitch is accurate.

Example 3n

Sometimes when soloing we focus on playing the changes, and sometimes we just blow over them. Here's an example of the latter.

Over the D chord in bar one, I just used the D Minor scale to create the melody. Launching with a Bb note is quite a dissonant choice. Supposing the D is a Dm chord, the Bb represents the #5 and implies a chord that is also sometimes written as Dm7b13. However, it creates a tension that is quickly resolved as we move to the root note on the B string.

In bar two, I essentially ignored the passing F chord and focused on G chord tones throughout. The high notes at the 17th fret make a G11 sound. Carried over into bar three over the D chord, they imply a D7#9 sound.

We can analyze these notes from a few perspectives, but our guide (whether we're trying to play the changes or just blowing) must be that it sounds good to us!

Example 3o

We end the solo on a climax with a busier line. In terms of the note choices, in bar one think D Major Pentatonic (D E F# A B) and in bar two G Mixolydian (G A B C D E F).

In bar three, we transition into the D Minor scale to bring a different flavor. Then we're back to G Mixolydian in bar four, with some quick chromatic passing notes added in, and in bar five we highlight the F# note to create a D Major vibe for the end of the line. It's worth noting again that I tend to think in terms of a pool of available notes that I can choose from. If you can visualize these intervals around chord shapes you already know, all the better.

Example 3p

Now here is the entire solo. Make it a project for your practice sessions to play the whole thing!

Example 3q – Full Solo

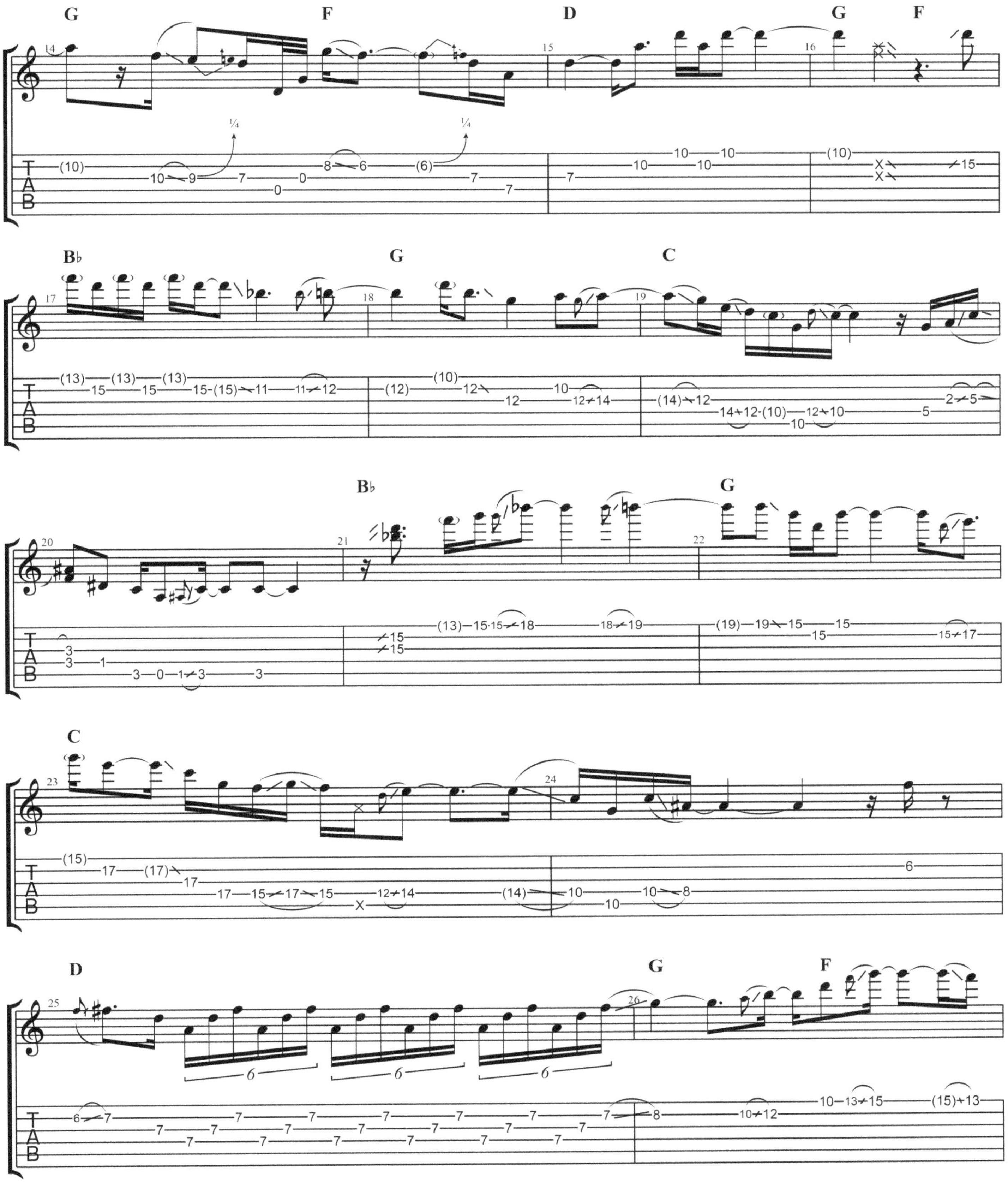
G F D G F
B♭ G C
B♭ G
C
D G F

D
G
F
D
G
F
D
G
F
D
G
F
D
(slide down slowly from random high notes)
G
F
D
G
F
D
G
F

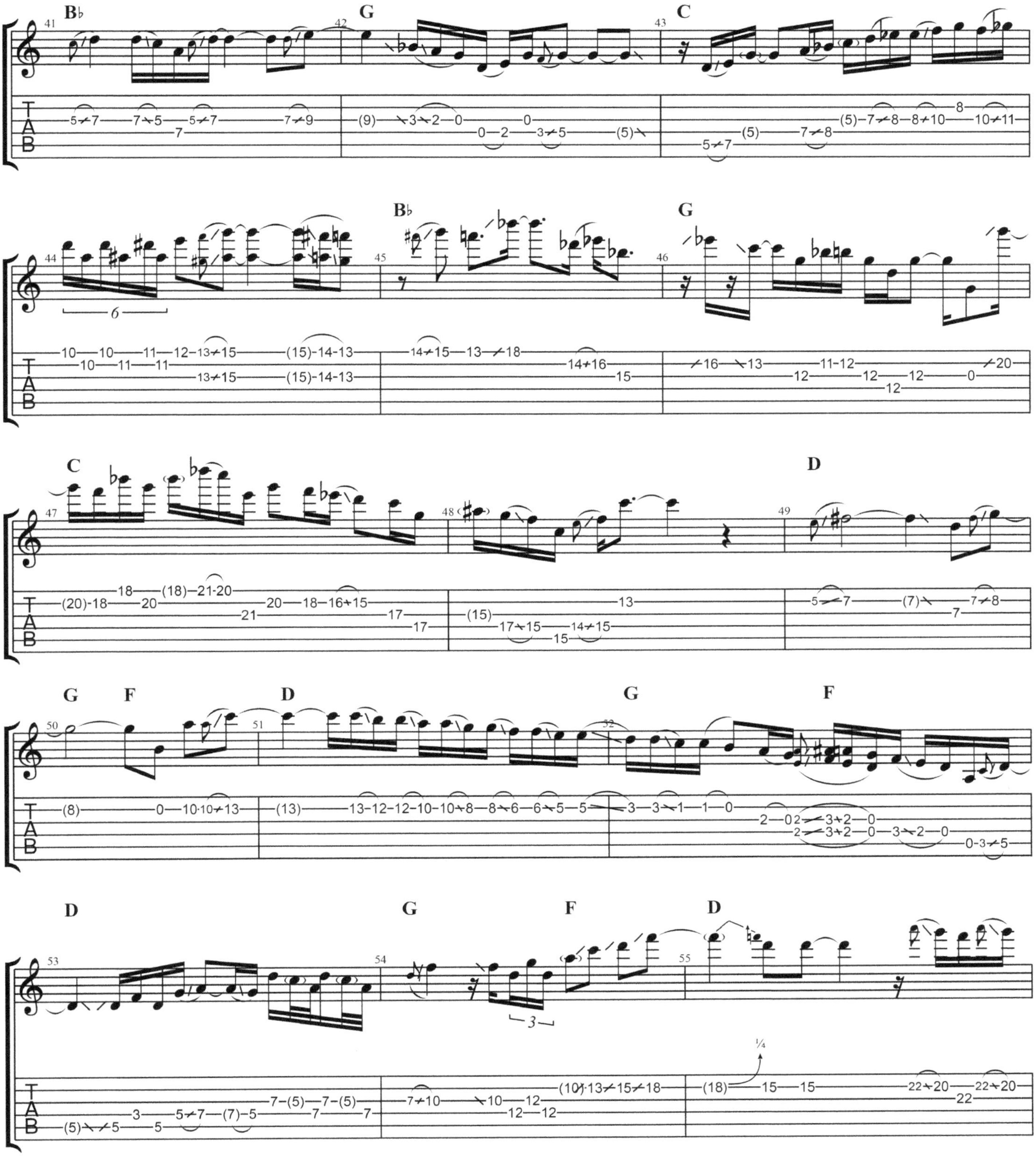
B♭
G
C
B♭
G
C
D
G
F
D
G
F
D
G
F
D

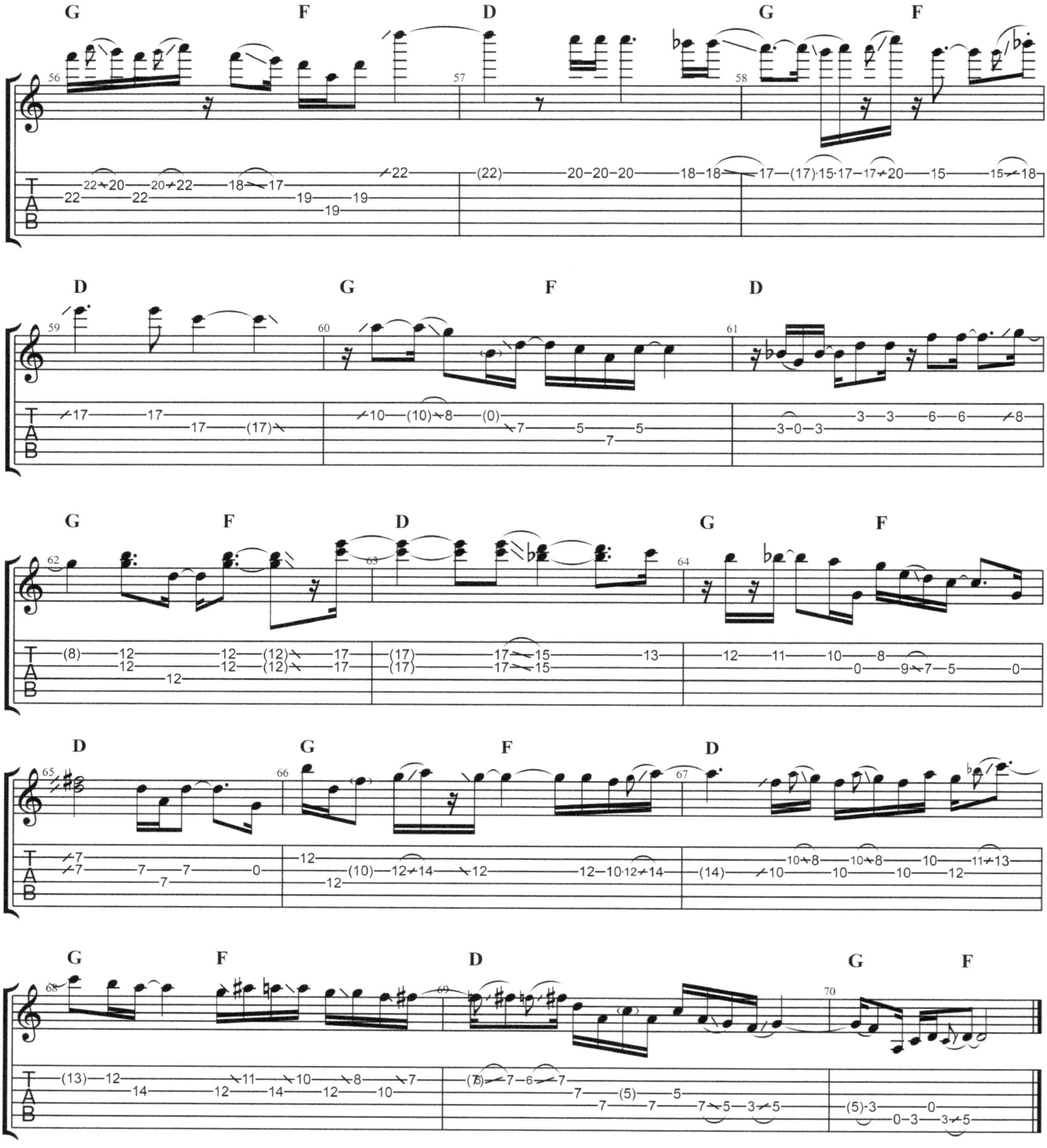
G F D G F
D G F D
G F D G F
D G F D
G F D G F

Chapter Four – New Orleans Funk Vamp Study

Modern blues-based music is influenced by other musical styles as well as pure blues, and these additional influences have given rise to a more fusion-blues based vocabulary.

I think of players like Josh Smith, whose playing has been influenced by jazz musicians such as Charlie Parker and Kenny Garrett, as well as the country guitarist Danny Gatton. All that music has informed his modern approach to blues playing.

Then there are players like Shane Theriot, who although not an out-and-out bluesman, digs into his New Orleans roots to add a funky, swampy, bluesy dimension to his playing.

Growing up in Alabama, I have those southern roots too, and in this chapter I want us to explore some ideas over a funky New Orleans style groove.

The influence of funk seeping into the blues has given rise to tunes that rely more on vamps, rather than the standard three-chord blues structure, so it's good to have some vocabulary ready to go for those one- or two-chord vamp scenarios that always come up in jam sessions!

One of the challenges of playing slide over this kind of groove is that slide playing is inherently legato, but here we want some syncopated grooving licks too. This makes excellent picking hand muting all the more necessary.

Example 4a serves as an introduction to the solo.

An E9 chord contains the notes E G# B D F#. In the pickup bar we target a G note, rather than G#, then push it slightly sharp and resolve to the E root note in bar one. The result is the effect of a bluesy bend.

In bar two, we mimic the syncopated guitar part to introduce some groove into this line. Make sure you mute the un-played strings really well.

Example 4a

This line is based around the E Mixolydian scale (E F# G# A B C# D).

Several times we also reference the G note from the E Minor Pentatonic scale, first as a chromatic approach note in bar one, then to simulate a minor to major bluesy bend.

In bar one, I play this opening phrase using the spare fingers behind the slide, then in bar two slide up into the 6th fret to play that phrase.

In bar three, you can play this whole phrase using the slide, but be sure to position it directly above the fret wire and don't add any vibrato. This will keep the note separation nice and clean.

Again, we're focusing on the minor 3rd (G) and sliding up and out of it to simulate a bend, which adds to the swampy feel of the line.

Example 4b

The previous eight bars formed a kind of intro, focusing on just the E9 chord. Now we switch to an E9 to A9 vamp.

When improvising over the backing track, it felt to me like the tune had properly begun at this point, so I decided to play a theme-like melody. It's a question and answer phrase, spread over four bars.

We start by targeting the root of the E9 chord on the top string.

In bar two, this phrase echoes the main guitar riff and ends on a D note. It's not a chord tone of A9 (A C# E G B) but creates an A9sus4 sound to add a little tension.

When the A9 comes around again, this time we play an F# note over it. This is an E Mixolydian scale note, and serves as an extended tone over A9 to create an A13sus4 sound.

Example 4c

We move on with a grooving motif-based line.

The main melodic idea is stated in full in bar one, then the subsequent bars play around with this idea.

Play the whole phrase in bar one just with the slide, maintaining good picking hand muting.

In bar two, slide into the notes at the 14th and 13th frets from below, then after playing parallel notes at the 14th, slide down to the 12th.

Focus on getting the articulation right to create some nice vocal phrasing.

Example 4d

In this line, we're focusing mostly on the E9 chord.

We start out with notes from E Mixolydian, but bar three is mostly E Minor Pentatonic, apart from the last couple of notes.

We acknowledge the presence of the A9 chord by simply targeting chord tones at the end of each phrase. At the beginning of bar two it's the A root note. At the beginning of bar four it's the 3rd (C#).

In bars 2-4, you'll play the majority of this long line with the slide, but the D note on the G string at the beginning of bar three (indicated with a bracket) is a fretted note played behind the slide.

Take a minute or two to plan out your fingering and slide movements across the fretboard.

Example 4e

This idea begins with one of my patented ascending triplet runs!

They are 1/16th note triplets and the line begins on the "e" of beat 3 (i.e., "1-e-&-a, 2-e-&-a, 3-**e**-&-a, 4-e-&-a").

This can be difficult to count, but listen to the audio a few times and it'll begin to feel like a natural starting point.

Notes at the 12th fret here are played behind the slide, which rests over fret 14 until we slide up in bar two.

The phrase at the end of bar four/beginning of bar five is syncopated and should pop out against the groove. Be careful to apply good muting.

Example 4f

This simple phrase highlights an E note throughout.

It's the root of the E9 chord, of course, but over A9 it's the 5th. Finding common notes in chords is always a good way to sound grounded in the harmony.

Example 4g

Here's a more complicated line that will take a little working out.

In bars 2-3, we have a very funky line that grooves, so after working out your fingering and slide movements, the main focal point for you will be timing.

The line is composed mostly of 1/16th notes, but at various points we punctuate it, either by adding a rest or an 1/8th note.

Breaking up the line in this way is what brings the groove (rather than playing a stream of 1/16th notes).

It's mostly E Mixolydian with one chromatic passing note on the B string thrown in, which also serves to help us change position on the neck.

This time, the ascending 1/16th note triplet run begins on the "a" of beat 1.

Example 4h

Example 4i draws on my Duane Allman influence and is a lick more typical of standard slide vocabulary. In bar one, start with the slide straight, parallel to the 12th fret.

To achieve this classic slide lick, pick the 12th fret of the B string then angle the slide to access the 10th fret. Then straighten the slide up again over the 12th.

Keep repeating this movement to get the B string slide from the 12th to the 10th, and return to the pedal tone at the 12th fret of the G string.

In bar two, angle the slide slightly to cover both the 15th and 16th frets. Moving from 1/16th notes to 1/16th note triplets in the latter half of the bar speeds up the lick.

In bar three, allow the notes to slur together, then slide down to the 14th fret.

Example 4i

The final part of the solo begins with a blues lick that again highlights the minor 3rd to create a moment of tension over the underlying major 3rd of the chord.

The tune ends as it began, over a static E9 vamp, so we're focusing mostly on the E Mixolydian scale here.

There are a couple of quick position shifts in this line, so be sure to plan out your movements before playing it.

Example 4j

Next, have a go at playing the entire solo. Use the backing track to jam over in your practice sessions.

Example 4k – Full Solo

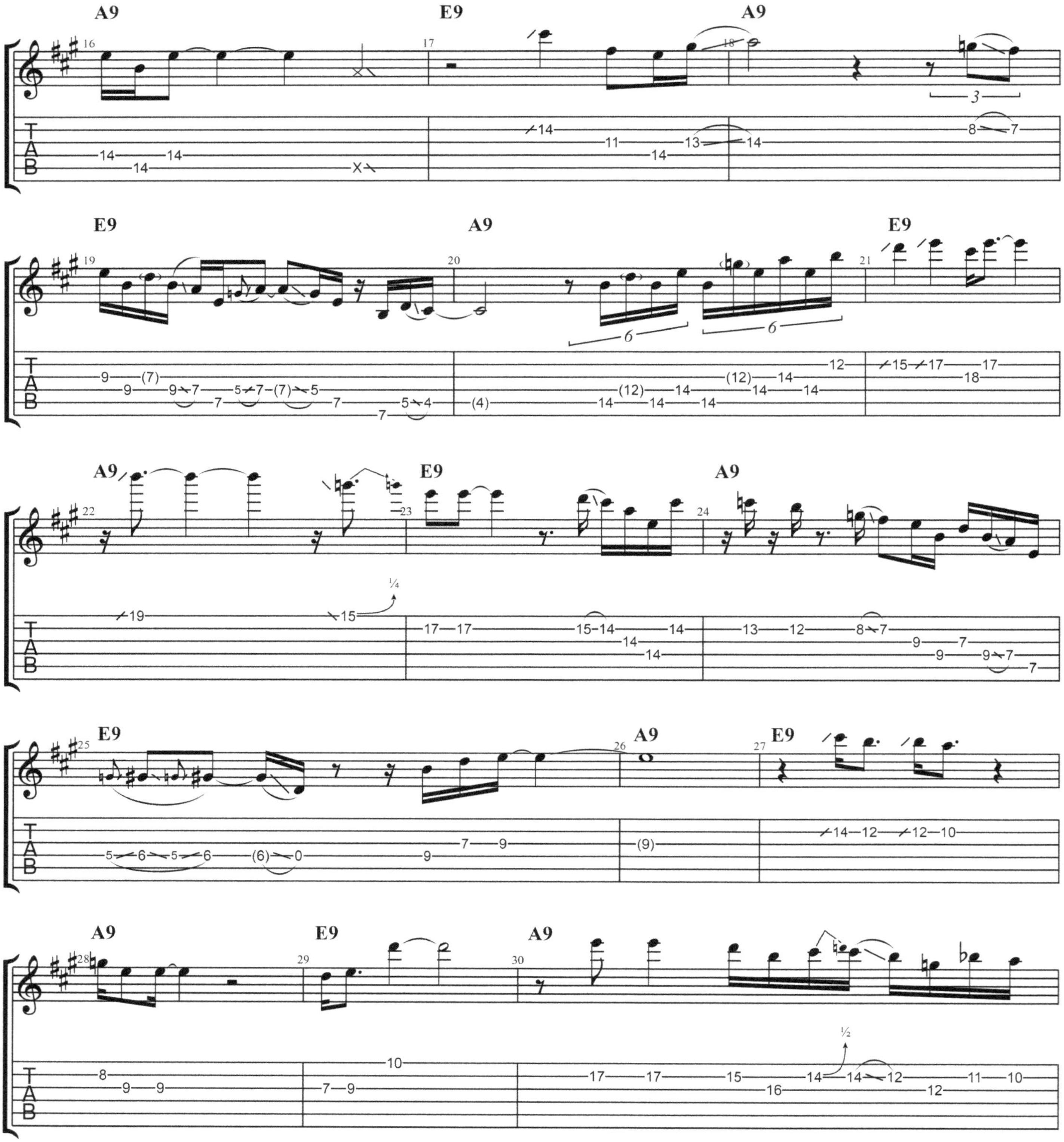
A9
E9
A9
E9
A9
E9
A9
E9
A9
E9
A9
E9
A9
E9
A9

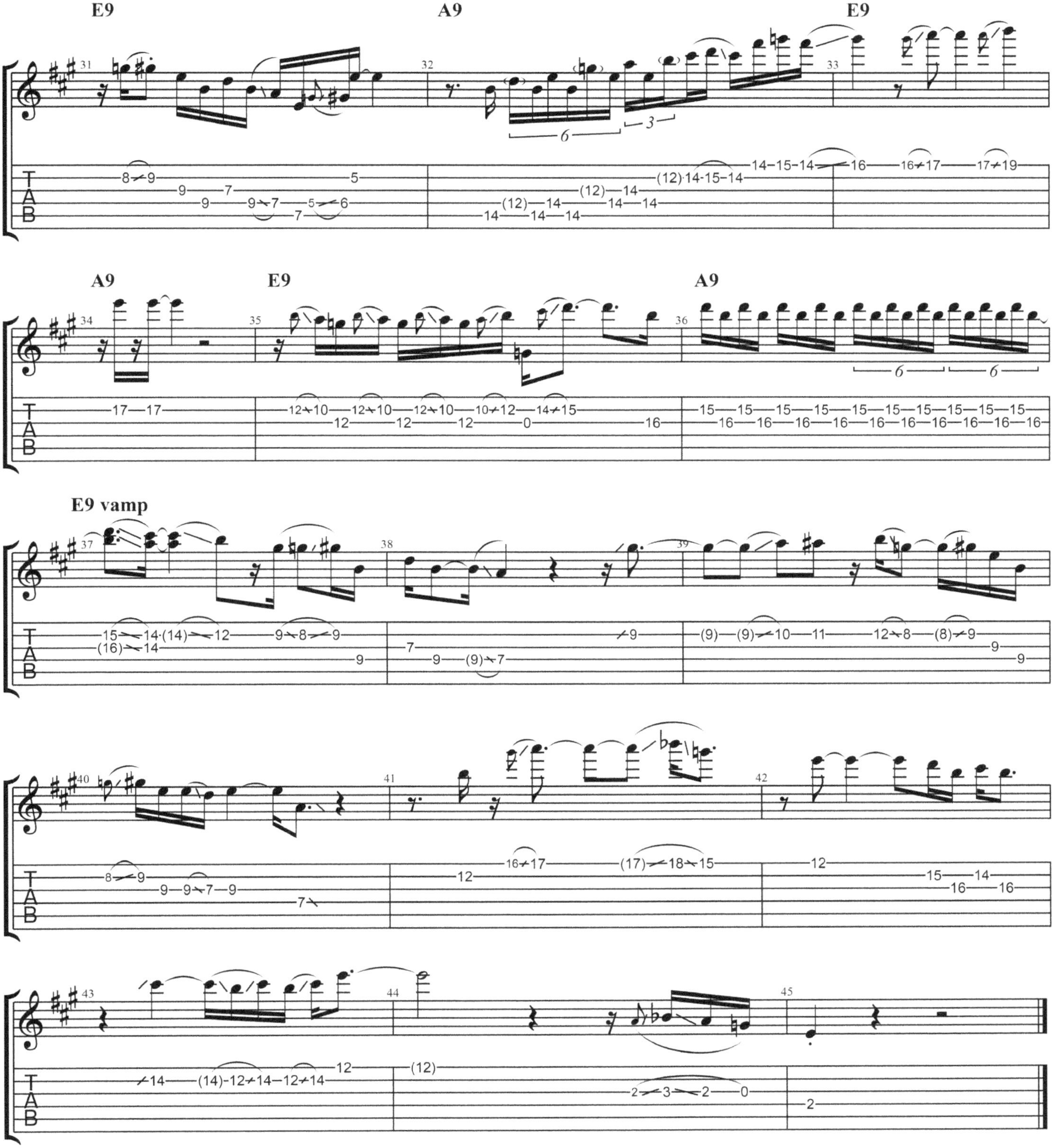
E9
A9
E9
A9
E9
A9
E9 vamp

Chapter Five – Modern Rock Study

In this final study, we're going to look at a modern rock tune that has a few more chord changes than the previous pieces. With a driving rock-based tune like this, it's easy to fall into clichés and play licks that have been heard many times before, especially those using pentatonic ideas. So, here our aim is to think more carefully about our notes choices and play ideas that are slightly more sophisticated.

Throughout, we will also be using this solo to continue to refine your slide pitching accuracy, vocal phrasing, dynamics, and all-important muting technique.

This tune is in the key of D Minor and all the chords belong to that key. However, the backing track uses a prominent riff throughout the A section which moves between D, F and C power chords.

Using only the root and 5th means that the tonality of those chords is ambiguous, and this opens up a number of melodic options for us. We can (and will!) flip between major and minor tonalities, drawing notes from major, Mixolydian and minor scales. In the B section (where we change to a Gm chord) the harmony is more defined, so our note choices will be more focused.

Example 5a replicates the main riff with the slide, adding some fills in between.

Example 5a

Although in the key of D Minor, for this example I chose to go for a D Mixolydian sound (D E F# G A B C).

Compared to the D Minor scale (D E F G A Bb C), D Mixolydian has a major 3rd (F#) and major 6th (B) – notes that provide a more uplifting mood.

The D Mixolydian scale still works over the C major chord in bar two, since it contains all the notes of a C major triad (C E G).

In bar two, slide into the 17th fret on the B string, angle your slide to access the 15th fret of the E string, then move back into position at the 17th fret for the rest of the lick.

In bars 3-4 we move away from D Mixolydian and play a couple of notes to outline the F and C chords.

Example 5b

To mark the change to the B section of the tune, we slide into a Gm chord, which we outline simply by playing its b3 (Bb) and 5th (D).

For the rest of this line I wanted to play something that sounded like a pre-composed, purposeful melody.

This whole section uses the D Minor scale. Although *all* of the chords in this tune occur naturally in the key of D Minor, we can use the ambiguous power chords of the A section to our advantage, and make scale choice decisions that sound like we're moving from a major tonality into the minor tonality of the B section.

I also used volume control swells to "fade" into certain notes, or "violining" as it used to be called, back in the day!

I use my pinky finger to manipulate the volume control on my guitar for this effect, but many readers will have a volume pedal as part of their effects setup, which is equally fine.

The effect draws the listener's attention to those melody notes and adds to the vocal phrasing effect.

Example 5c

As the B section chords repeat, we conclude the melodic phrasing idea. Things are about to get heavy again with the driving riff section, so in anticipation of that we need to generate some energy to carry us into the A section, setting us up to play more dynamic lines.

Here, we achieve that by including a 1/16th note triplet passage that resolves to an F chord. As we've seen throughout our studies, introducing 1/16th note triplets over a straight 4/4 beat has the effect of speeding up a line. It's a great "energy generator" that we can use as a springboard for other ideas.

To play the lick in bar two, make sure you effectively mute all the strings apart from the G and D.

Use your slide to play the notes at the 5th fret, rolling the slide off to sound the open G string. Do the same for the Bb note at the 3rd fret.

Use your thumb and first finger to play the G and D strings. The palm of your fretting hand should be muting the low E and A strings, and your spare fingers muting the B and high E. When you slide from the 3rd fret into the 2nd, pluck both strings together to sound the F chord.

Take a similar approach to play the lick in bar three, which this time utilizes three open strings.

Example 5d

As we move back into the A section and the energy ramps up, here's a more complex line for you.

Let's break it down.

In bar one, the opening phrase hints at the main riff, then a triplet passage leads into the C chord in bar two. By now you can probably identify from the TAB exactly how the triplet phrase should be played from a technical point of view. The slide will remain in place at the 12th fret, and notes at the 10th will be fretted behind the slide.

In bar three we land on the C chord with a G note (the 5th). For the lick that occupies the rest of the bar, capturing that vocal articulation is important. Slide into the 12th fret from above, then slide back up to the 14th in order to slide back down to the 10th. It's just three simple notes on one string, but the articulation breathes life into the phrase.

The end of the phrase in bar two is targeting a D root note at the beginning of bar three. From there, we employ a similar strategy as before: a climbing triplet lick targets a C major chord tone. But this time, the triplet lick spans all the strings from the A string to the high E.

To get this lick sounding clean, pick adjacent strings with your thumb and first finger. Then, instead of trying to use your other fingers for the higher strings, just move your picking hand across the strings, allowing your palm and fingers to mute any un-played strings.

When you reach the notes on the top string, pluck these using upstrokes with the first finger. You'll hear that over the C chord in bar four, we're playing a bluesy D Mixolydian lick for a change of flavor.

Example 5e

For the repeat of the A section, here's a descending idea. The lick that begins on the last note of bar one and crosses into bar two uses an adapted version of one of our foundational licks.

Here, rather than sliding into a note from above on one string, then sliding into a second note on an adjacent string from below, you'll slide into the first note from above, then jump position with your slide to play the adjacent string. It's a subtle change in technique, but this tweak gives more separation between the notes and allows us to focus on the initial slurred note.

The phrase in bars 3-4 mimics the underlying power chord riff.

Example 5f

Back in the B section, here's a repeating lick over the Gm chord that you'll have no problem executing by this stage. The slide is at the 15th fret, and notes behind the slide at the 13th are played with the first finger.

In bar two, after the first four notes you'll move the slide out of position briefly before sliding back to the 15th.

In bar three, this is a staple blues lick adapted for slide. Notes on the G string are played with the thumb, and notes on the high E with the second finger. The first finger's job here is to sound the open B string notes in between.

Example 5g

In this B section idea, we are playing with some extended note color over the Gm chord, as we cycle between its Bb chord tone (b3) and an A note. The A note is the 9th of Gm, implying a Gm9 sound.

Listen to the audio to get the feel of this opening lick. You're aiming to get a "crying" or "wailing" sound with your articulation.

In the latter half of bar one, we introduce some tension by adding a single chromatic passing note (Ab) between chord tones, leading into the Bb chord at the beginning of bar two, landing on its 3rd (D).

Making a motif out of the idea, we repeat the melodic line from bar one at the end of bar two. This time we leave out the chromatic note and, as the line crosses into bar three, we need to adjust the ending to fit over the F chord, which we do by playing its 5th.

The main idea of these phrases on the B string is to achieve a very vocal-like sound by picking once, then moving the slide between the notes. Listen to the audio and you'll get the idea.

It's the kind of articulation technique that is often used by Derek Trucks and the Nashville-based slide player M.P. Gannon.

It does, of course, call for great accuracy with your intonation, as you seek to move seamlessly between the notes.

Example 5h

In Example 5i, for a change of scene we're playing the D Blues scale (D F G Ab A C) over bars 1-2. The rest of this line locks back into the main riff. Add plenty of articulation to the high notes.

Example 5i

Example 5j is the conclusion of the solo.

Leading into the D chord, the fast ascending triplet lick in the pickup bar is an adaptation of what we've played before.

Normally, the lick is confined to adjacent strings, or it will move across the strings playing strings in pairs. Instead, here we introduce a string skip, using the A note on the D string as a pedal tone. The slide is held at the 19th fret for most of this lick, and the notes at the 17th are fretted behind it.

This little idea is tricky to execute cleanly and presents a picking challenge, so I recommend slowing it right down and getting all the mechanical aspects in place before attempting it at tempo.

You'll begin with your first finger on the G string, 17th fret, with the slide playing notes on the D string, 19th fret. After the first six notes, hop your first finger over onto the B string, 17th fret, leaving the slide in place.

Next, the slide will need to move to the 20th fret to play the note on the B string, while your first finger moves onto the high E.

In bar two, you're aiming to introduce some drama with a quick slide, followed by a note played over the neck pickup. We're targeting the root of the F chord, but adding lots of vibrato.

To end, the lick works its way down the neck to end on the root of the C chord.

Example 5j

Now that you've practiced all the individual lines in this solo, see if you can begin to put them together. Here's the whole solo notated. As always, use the backing track to jam out your own ideas and compose your own slide licks.

Example 5k – Full Solo

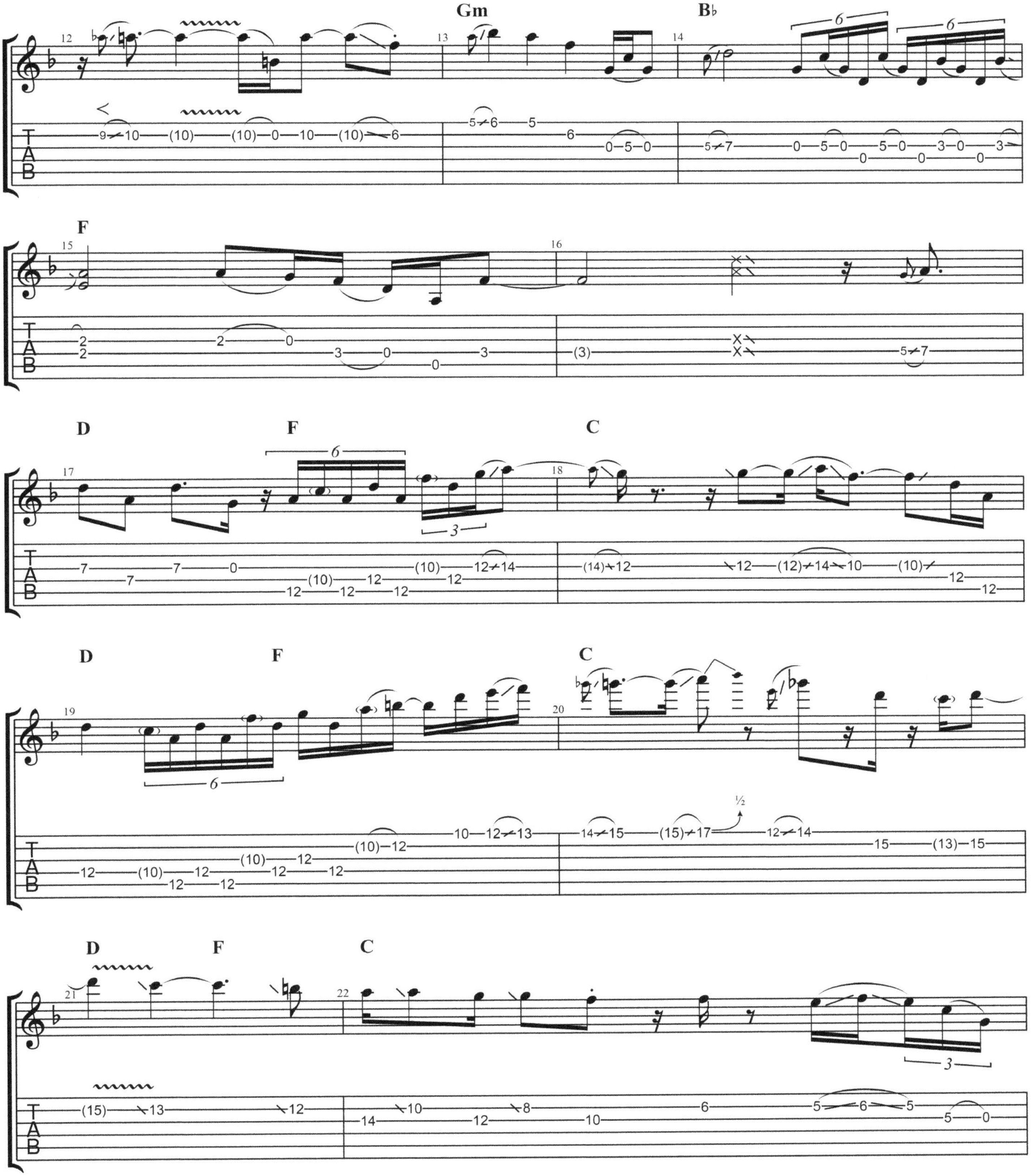
Gm
B♭
F
D
F
C
D
F
C
D
F
C

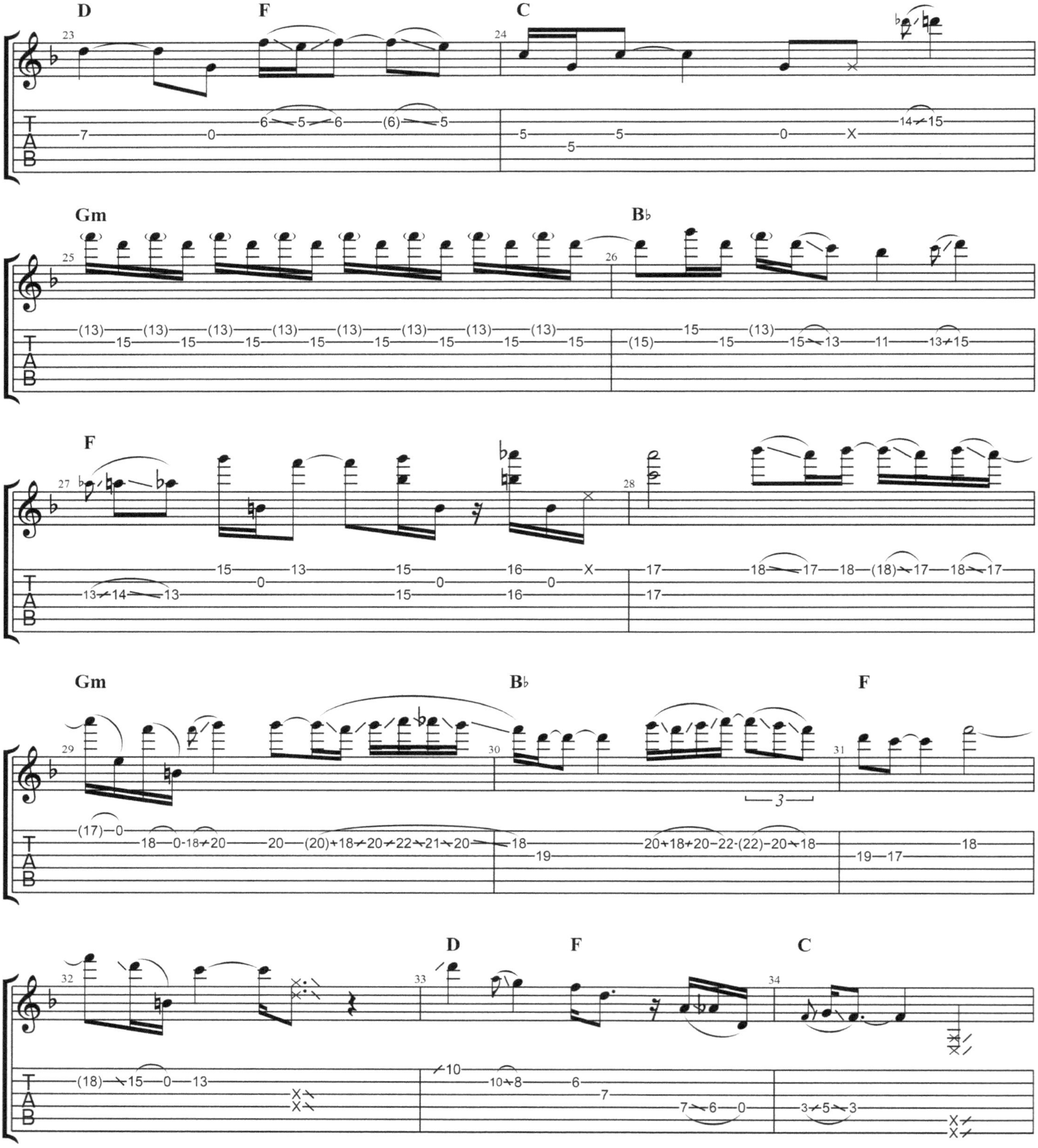
D
F
C
Gm
B♭
F
Gm
B♭
F
D
F
C

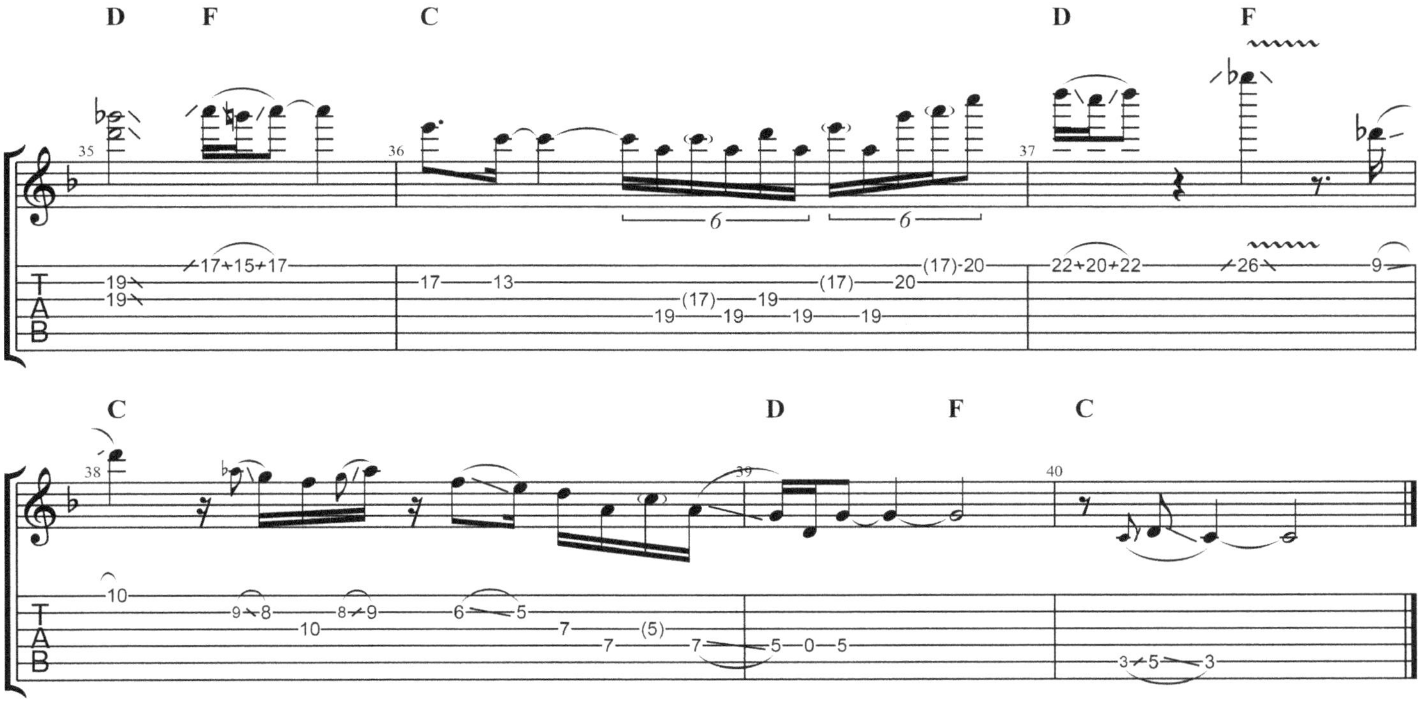
D F C D F
C D F C

Conclusion

I hope you've enjoyed this look at the possibilities that playing slide in standard tuning can give us. If you're a fan of modern blues music, you'll know that there are times when only a slide solo will do! But it's great to have the flexibility to pick up the slide and use it without having to retune or change to a different guitar.

From here, continue to work on the core technical aspects of your slide playing:

- Great intonation and pitching accuracy

- Note control and vocal articulation

- Excellent picking hand muting to produce a clear sound

And also practice the foundational lick techniques we've looked at:

- Sliding in different directions on adjacent strings

- Playing phrases that include fretted notes behind the slide

- Playing blues curls with the slide

- Using angled slide licks

- Rhythmic licks that cut across the groove

- Special effect licks like playing notes beyond the end of the fretboard and moving harmonics

Have fun using the backing tracks from this book and work on your slide phrasing in your practice times. If you're able, record yourself and listen back. This is always a revealing (sometimes horrifying, at first) process. Especially when we realize, "Wow, my muting sucks – listen to all those ringing strings!" or "Gee, I need to tighten up my timing." But it's the best and quickest way to identify and fix areas of weakness in our playing, and also to discover the things that we like and should focus on more in our playing.

Have fun and enjoy your music.

Allen.

About the Author

A native of Auburn, Alabama, Allen was exposed to blues and R&B at an early age. Moving into jazz and fusion in his teens, he attended Berklee College of Music and, shortly after, moved to Los Angeles on a scholarship through *Guitar Player Magazine* to attend the Musicians Institute, where he has remained on staff to the present day.

Allen has six solo CDs to his name and his version of Michael McDonald's *I Keep Forgettin' (Every Time You're Near)* is shooting up the charts at the time of writing, and can be heard often on Sirius FM radio. His recordings feature an amazing array of musicians, including Jimmy Johnson, Vinnie Coaliuta, Abraham Laboriel, Genevieve Artadi, Maxayn Lewis, Jeff Babko, Dave Hooper, Matt Rhodi, J.V. Collier, Randy Crawford, Tolak Olestaad, Jimmy Earl, Jimmy Haslip, Will Kennedy, Reinhardt Melz, Mark McMilllen, Roberto Vally, Dave Hughes, Hanz Zermuellan, Joey Heredia, Brian Simpson and others.

Also check out his work on the Wonderland Park album *Just Get In*, and *Held to a Different Standard* with Brad Rabuchin. Allen's music can be heard on Spotify and also many cable TV shows, such as *Sons of Guns, Pawn Stars, Duck Dynasty, Build it Bigger,* National Geographic specials, and more.

Besides his solo career, and being a regular featured artist in *Guitar Techniques*, *Guitarist,* and other magazines, Allen has published several instructional courses. His book *Liquid Legato* was published by Musicians Institute in collaboration with Hal Leonard, and his popular *Fusion Blues Guitar Soloing* book by Fundamental Changes. In addition, his Melodic Improv video course is available on TrueFire.

Allen has performed and/or recorded with jazz and R&B luminaries including Hiroshima, Randy Crawford, Gino Vannelli, Patti Austin, Roberta Flack, Stevie Wonder, Jon Waite, BeBe and CeCe Winans, The Crusaders, Bobby Caldwell, James Ingram, Joan Baez and many, many others.

By the Same Author

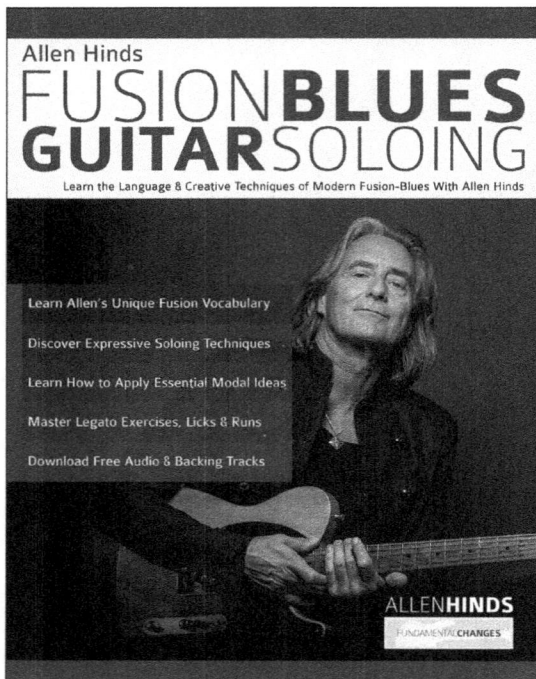

Master modern fusion-blues guitar with virtuoso Allen Hinds

Stuck in a rut with your blues guitar?

Ready to go beyond blues guitar and introduce modern fusion elements to your playing?

Allen Hinds is respected internationally for his mastery of the fusion-blues genre. As "the players' teacher" he has guided countless guitar students to success as the instructor and artist in residence at the Musicians Institute in Hollywood. His playing credits include *Natalie Cole, The Crusaders, Eric Marienthal, James Ingram, Randy Crawford, Marc Antoine* and many more.

In **Fusion Blues Guitar Soloing** he passes his mastery on to you! Along with bespoke drills and technique building exercises, you'll learn dozens of original licks as Allen solos over a selection of tracks created especially for this book.

What You'll Learn

Fusion Blues Guitar Soloing will help you discover the theory, technique and lyrical melodic approach that makes Allen such a compelling, in-demand player. By the end of the book, you will have mastered his musical ideas and be using them fluently to create your own blazing solos.

Phase 1 – **Three Essential Modes**

Allen explains his revolutionary approach to *properly* getting creative with the Ionian, Dorian and Mixolydian modes. When used properly, you'll see that you don't need a million exotic scales to sound exciting. In fact, you'll discover how to apply any lick "modally" and make it work in a range of different harmonic situations.

Phase 2 – **How to Build Solos with Motifs**

Allen shares his secrets to developing motival ideas that start small and build in complexity. When you master this approach, all your solos will tell meaningful stories to your audience.

- Learn how to take a simple motif and transpose it through a parent scale

- Apply motifs across string sets

- Discover more modern intervallic motifs

- Learn fantastic motif-driven licks and a full-length solo

Phase 3 – **Mastering Legato Technique**

Allen is constantly asked to teach the secrets of his iconic legato technique. In this section you'll discover…

- Core exercises to strengthen the fretting hand

- How to achieve beautiful, fluid legato phrasing

- Precise left and right-hand coordination

- How to use legato as a creative force in your music

Phase 4 – **Create Innovative Solos with Major, Minor and Dominant Grooves**

In the final three chapters of the book, things get taken to a whole new level as Allen teaches some monster solos. Rocking, funky, and soulful blues tracks showcase dozens of fantastic, innovative licks you can add to your vocabulary. It's masterclass in soloing and harmonic mastery and all broken down step-by-step!

Hear It!

Bonus 1: This book comes with studio quality audio FREE to download, so you can hear exactly how each exercise, lick and solo sounds.

Bonus 2: Backing tracks of each tune used in the book, so you can practice licks and solos.